HOW TO
PREPARE YOUR
MANUSCRIPT FOR
A PUBLISHER

HOW TO PREPARE YOUR MANUSCRIPT FOR A PUBLISHER

David L. Carroll

PARAGON HOUSE
New York

Published in the United States by

Paragon House
90 Fifth Avenue
New York, NY 10011

10 9 8 7 6 5

Library of Congress Cataloging-in-Publication Data

Carroll, David L.
   How to prepare your manuscript for a publisher /
David L. Carroll.

      p.   cm.
   ISBN 1-55778-131-1
   1. Manuscript preparation (Authorship)   I. Title.
PN160.C34 1988
808' .02—dc19   88-2446

Manufactured in the United States of America

Contents

Part I. Getting a Book Contract

1. Submitting Manuscripts   3
    1.1 What is an Unsolicited
         Manuscript?   3
    1.2 Target Your Market   4
    1.3 How to Write a Persuasive
         Query Letter   5
    1.4 Methods of Submission: The
         Manuscript and the Proposal   6

1.5 The Question of an Agent   12

1.6 Questions and Answers about
     Submissions   14

Part II. Preparing Your Manuscript

2. Manuscript Presentation   23

   2.1 Paper   23

   2.2 Typing   24

   2.3 Margins and Spacing   24

   2.4 Manuscript Length   24

   2.5 Page Numbering   25

   2.6 Front Matter   26

   2.7 Table of Contents   27

   2.8 Mounting Reprint Copy   27

   2.9 Making On-page Corrections   28

3. Style   29

   3.1 Spelling   29

   3.2 Capitalization   30

   3.3 Hyphenation   33

   3.4 Emphasis   34

   3.5 Foreign Words   34

   3.6 Numbers   35

   3.7 Technical and Mathematical
      Copy   38

3.8   Subheadings   39
3.9   Endnotes   40
3.10 Bibliographies   42
3.11 Index   44
3.12 Tables   45
3.13 Cross-references   47
3.14 Quotations   47
3.15 Racism, Obscenities, Crude
      Language   49
3.16 Sexist Language   49
3.17 Using Style Guide Reference
      Books   51

4. Drawings, Photographs, Charts, and
   Graphs   52
   4.1 Permissions, Fees, and
        Credits   52
   4.2 Preparing the Illustrations   54
   4.3 Submission and Return of Art
        Materials   56

5. Responsibilities of Editors of
   Contributed Volumes   58

6. Delivering the Final Manuscript   62

Part III. Production and Publication of Your Manuscript

7. Preparing Your Manuscript for
   Publication   67
   7.1 The Copyedited Manuscript   67
   7.2 Answering the Editor's
       Queries   70
   7.3 Reading and Correcting the
       Galleys   70
   7.4 Alteration Charges to the
       Author   72
   7.5 Selling Rights to Your Book   72

Part IV. Legal Concerns for Authors

8. Copyright   77
   8.1 What is Copyright?   77
   8.2 What Does a Copyright
       Protect?   78

9. Permissions   80
   9.1 Responsibility for Permissions   80
   9.2 Getting Permissions   80
   9.3 When Permission is Denied   84

10. Fair Use   85
   10.1 The Limits of Fair Use   85
   10.2 Speeches, Interviews,
        Newspaper Copy   87
   10.3 What Constitutes Libel?   88

Part V. Special Concerns

11. Converting the Thesis into Book
    Form   93
   11.1 Tone   93
   11.2 Style   94

12. Guidelines for the Use of Word
    Processors   97
   12.1 Do's and Don'ts on the
        Computer   97
   12.2 Printers   100

Suggested Readings   101

Part I

GETTING A BOOK CONTRACT

1
Submitting Manuscripts

1.1 WHAT IS AN UNSOLICITED MANUSCRIPT?

An unsolicited manuscript is a manuscript that is neither requested nor commissioned nor sold through a middleperson, i.e., an agent or occasionally, a lawyer or business manager. Usually it is written on an uncommissioned basis, then submitted to a publisher directly by the author. The publisher reads the manuscript and responds with a yes or a no.

How difficult is it to get an unsolicited manuscript published? Difficult—especially if you have no personal contacts at a publisher's office and if you are submitting your work cold. It is, however, by no means an impossibility, especially if your manuscript is a competent and significant piece of work. The next few pages will tell you how to maximize your chances.

1.2 TARGET YOUR MARKET

Before sending out an unsolicited manuscript make sure the subject matter of your book is correctly matched to the publisher's fields of specialization. It will, for example, do an author no good to send a manuscript on equitation to a company which specializes in books on East European politics. Yet, it is surprising how often writers send the hard-earned fruits of their labors to an inappropriate publisher, not spending the small amount of research time it takes to locate the right home for the right material.

A real aid in this direction will be to consult a copy of *Writer's Market*, published each year by Writer's Digest Books. This volume is obtainable at the reference section of any good library or bookstore. *Writer's Market* presents a detailed list of book publishers in America along with their fields of specialization, addresses, editor's names, and office numbers. A work that offers a similar service is LMP *(Literary Market*

Place), available at most libraries and some book stores.

1.3 HOW TO WRITE A PERSUASIVE QUERY LETTER

Once you have compiled a list of promising publishers, save time and possible disappointment by writing to them directly, describing your book and inquiring if they are interested. Some publishers simply do not accept unsolicited works; others may be short of readers at the present time, or they may currently not be taking on new projects. Find out first.

Query letters should not be lengthy, but should provide substantial information concerning what your book is about, as well as who will buy the book and why. Describe your book's main subject, its premise, story, research sources, special features, and important conclusions. Explain what gaps the book will fill, what makes it special, and why its publication will profit the publisher. If you are going to interview people, identify them. If you plan to travel for this book, say where. How soon can you deliver the manuscript? How many pages will it contain? If you have access to new, unusual, or provocative research materials, send along a few xeroxed examples. Finally, put in a moderate amount of information about your writing experience. Remember, you are selling both yourself and your book in this letter. Make it informative, literate, not more than a page-and-a-half long, and nicely to the point.

A good query letter should function like advertising copy; it should make the reader curious to experience the product.

Most publishers will respond to query letters within a few weeks. If they show interest the next step is to send them your submission.

1.4 METHODS OF SUBMISSION: THE MANUSCRIPT AND THE PROPOSAL

Submissions to publishers take two forms:

1) A completed book manuscript.
2) A book proposal.

1. The Completed Book Manuscript

A. *Manuscript Appearance*. All completed book manuscripts should be typed (double-spaced) on standard white bond using 8½-by-11-inch typing paper—no hand-written submissions, ever! All pages should be of uniform size.

Avoid typing on onion skin, or on coated, erasable papers. Office machine copies of a manuscript are acceptable as long as they are clear and not too darkly reproduced. Manuscripts printed on a NLQ (Near Letter Quality) dot matrix printer are also usually acceptable.

B. Shipping. Manuscripts should be placed in an appropriate wrapping and mailed First Class or Parcel Post directly to the publisher (see section 6, "Delivering the Final Manuscript"). Be sure to include a cover letter providing your name, address, phone number, and any appropriate explanations that may be necessary and a stamped, self addressed envelope. Along with this you should also provide the following information:

- A comparison of other books in the field which may compete with your book, along with an analysis of how your book is better/more worthwhile/more up-to-date than the others.
- A run-down of possible markets for the book. Where does your book fit within the competitive environment? Who will buy it? Libraries? Colleges? Clubs? Businesses? Experts? Scholars?

Specific organizations? Can it be used as a textbook? Might it become required reading for a college course? Will it have a trade audience or a general readership? What about mail order? Are there specialized markets that will purchase copies? Be sure to be as specific as possible here. Avoid vague, general statements that are less believable than specific ones.

· A resume or curriculum vitae (no longer than three pages).

Finally, be sure to keep a duplicate copy of the complete manuscript for your files. Though publishers usually make all efforts to protect manuscripts, accidents happen.

C. Manuscript Evaluation. Once received, your manuscript will be read by an in-house editor or sent to one or more professional readers for evaluation. Final assessments will usually be made by the reader(s) on the following grounds:

· Depth, importance, and interest of subject matter.
· Originality and/or topicality of concept and idea.
· Quality of writing style.

· The book's potential market-
ability.

As a rule, publishers accept or reject a
manuscript within a month or two after submission. Occasionally, manuscripts will be kept for
several months, especially if they must be eval-
uated by more than one reader. If you do not
receive acceptance or rejection after, say, three
months, you certainly have a right to get in
touch with the publisher and inquire after the
whereabouts of your manuscript.

D. Presentation. A word on neatness: a sur-
prisingly large number, perhaps even a majority
of submissions (both solicited and unsolicited),
come to publishers in a state of sloppy disarray.
While staff readers generally try to give each
project a fair evaluation, a creased, poorly
typed, badly punctuated, heavily corrected,
and/or improperly paginated manuscript cannot
help but slow down the reading process and pos-
sibly prejudice the reader in your disfavor.

2. The Book Proposal

When submitting a book proposal to a publisher
it is standard procedure to include the following
sections:

· A detailed outline explaining

what your book is about, its
theme, narrative line, purpose,
and the type of research and/or
personal experience you will use
to support it. Outlines should
run no longer than three or four
pages.
- A proposed table of contents.
This section can be combined
with or interwoven into the
outline.
- A sample chapter. Be sure this
chapter contains materials that is
central to the main topic of your
book. Send only principal chapters; do not submit introductions
or conclusions. Sample chapters
should generally run from fifteen
to thirty double-spaced pages.
- An analysis of other books in the
field which compete with your
book, plus an explanation of how
your book is better/more to the
point/more insightful/more up-
to-date than the others. What
the editor is looking for here
are "selling handles," phrases,
"buzzwords," concepts that can
be featured in presentation of

the book to salespeople at sales conferences, in a two or three minute pitch to the bookstore manager or buyer for a chain of bookstores, in a catalog writeup, or in a direct mail piece.

· A description of possible markets. Where does your book fit within the competitive environment? Who will buy it? Libraries? Colleges? Clubs? Businesses? Experts in the field? Scholars? Specific organizations? Can it be used as a text book? Might it become required reading for a college course? Will it have a trade audience or a general readership? What about mail order? Are there specialized markets that will purchase copies?

· A resume or curriculum vitae (no longer than three pages).

All of the above (20 to 40 pages is a typical length for a proposal) is sent directly to the publisher. Evaluation time usually takes from four to eight weeks.

1.5 THE QUESTION OF AN AGENT

Manuscripts can be sent to publishers in two ways: from the author or via an agent. Most unsolicited manuscripts come from authors, most solicited manuscripts from agents. But is there really such a thing as a "solicited" manuscript? And is an agent really necessary?

Yes and no to both questions. Solicited simply means that good agents will know what type of materials publishers are currently searching for, and they will be able to direct your manuscript to these targeted areas. The advantages of having an agent are, first, that good agents work hard at cultivating editors and often have direct access to these key players whenever they wish to peddle a particular project. Publishers, at the same time, are more likely to pay attention to proposals and manuscripts that come directly from an agency, especially if they know and deal with this agency on a regular basis. This fact alone can give you a hefty advantage over the competition. Another plus is that an agent negotiates all contractual matters with the publisher. Since a share of the profits goes into his or her pocket, the agent will naturally try to get you the best advance, rights, and royalty deals possible.

On the down side, most agents charge 10 or

15 percent for their efforts, and this can add up. If, for example, you receive $10,000 for a literary property, the actual amount of cash that reaches your pocket after the agent takes a 15 percent cut will be only $8500.

Big agencies also tend to give priority to their more established clients, which can create difficulties for the first-time author.

Still, an agent can be a powerful ally and will more often than not bolster your cause— but only if you can get one in the first place. If you're thinking of going the agent route, start by consulting a copy of *LMP (Literary Market Place)*. It contains an exhaustive list of literary agencies *and* a list of titles they specialize in (some agents handle only fiction, others computer books, self-help, romantic novels, fashion, cookbooks, etc.).

When you find several agencies that seem well-suited to your needs, send a letter of inquiry. If you receive a positive reply, mail your manuscript or proposal to the agency directly, along with a cover letter, making sure to enclose a check, money order, or stamped envelope to defray return costs. Start with the smaller agents, or with an agent who is just beginning in the field, or an agent based outside of New York City, which is where most of the biggest literary agents operate. He or she will have fewer clients at the start and will be more likely to accept the work of unpublished or little-published authors. Do be careful, however, of agencies that promise to read your manuscript for a fee. Some literary organizations extract a tidy side income this way, and the proportion of manuscripts they accept is usually miniscule compared to the number read and charged for.

1.6 QUESTIONS AND ANSWERS ABOUT SUBMISSIONS

The following questions are frequently asked by prospective authors.

Can I submit my graduate thesis for publication?

Yes, publishers receive many thesis submissions every year. Although most of these turn out to be too specialized or too scholarly for publication, certain choice works do sometimes end up on a publisher's list. If you *are* submitting a thesis it is a good idea first to tailor it for a more popular readership. Your best shot with a thesis, even after broadening its focus, is a university press or a privately owned scholarly house. See *Literary Market Place* for listings.

Can I make more than one submission at a time?

You can, within reason, submit as many ideas, proposals, or manuscripts as you like to a publisher. However, most publishers consider projects one at a time: finish your first book and you usually can go on to the second. Moreover, if your first submission is rejected, write the publisher concerning other book ideas you're contemplating and the publishers will usually let you know if they wish to see a formal proposal.

Can I submit a partially completed manuscript?

Yes. Be sure and accompany it with a proposal, as described in section 1.3 "How to Write a Persuasive Query Letter" above, an outline of the unfinished sections, and a complete table of contents.

How will I be notified if my book is accepted or rejected?

If your manuscript is rejected the publisher will return it to you by mail, usually within four to eight weeks. If it is accepted they will let you know directly, by phone, by letter, or through your agent. If you are using an agent be sure he or she keeps you informed of the manuscript's progress on at least a quasi-regular basis.

After the book is accepted, what then?

The publisher will arrange an editorial meeting with you in their offices or, if you live at a distance, over the phone. At this meeting you will agree on the details of the book's organization, content, and style. Then contracts will be drawn up, sent to you, and signed. Now you go to work.

Once the publisher has your completed manuscript it will be sent out for copyediting, then printed in galleys, then shipped to you for final corrections (see section 7, "Preparing Your Manuscript for Publication"). The whole publication process usually takes from nine to twelve months, depending on the book, particularly on how large an art program (photographs, line drawings, charts, tables) it has. When the matter of time is involved, opt for the conservative estimate and plan on seeing your work in print approximately one year after you hand in the finished copy.

Will I work with an editor?

Yes, at the beginning of the project the publisher will assign you an in-house editor who will be available for consultation and editorial advice throughout the writing of the book, and then again during the book's production. Your editor will ordinarily be able to answer all questions concerning writing style and editorial procedure.

How and when will I be paid?

Once publishers have accepted your manuscript or proposal, they will offer you an advance against royalties. If the offer is acceptable you will receive part (usually half) of the advance upon signing, part upon completion of the manuscript. Specific royalty arrangements will be discussed with you directly during negotiations and spelled out in the contract.

How much time will I be given to write the book?

Each book is different. One year is a representative length of time, though the deadline will sometimes be longer, sometimes shorter, depending on the nature of the project. Publishers usually prefer not to go to contract on a book which is more than three years away from manuscript delivery.

What reference style manual should I consult when preparing my manuscript?

There are many. You will find the best of them in the reference section of any library or good book store. *The Chicago Manual of Style* and *Words Into Type* are especially popular these days with major publishers.

How will the publisher promote my book?

This depends entirely on the publisher. As a rule, if the publisher maintains their initial excitement about a book and thinks it is a commercial winner, they will advertise it and push their salesmen to market it aggressively. For particularly important books authors may be sent on a one- or two-week author's tour, though it is primarily the larger companies that can afford to do this on a regular basis.

Publishers are often shorthanded when it comes to promoting their books. There are 50,000 new titles published every year; half of these are intended for the retail store. Publishers by necessity often operate on a "bird out of the nest" theory—i.e., throw the book out there and see if it flies. Since their marketing budgets are limited, they must be extremely selective about where they put their money, and which books to support. It usually boils down to the books that can do the most business getting the most marketing support. An author can help by volunteering his or her services for a publicity tour, soliciting favorable endorsements from experts or celebrities, or making the rounds of the book stores, introducing oneself and talking up one's book. Your best point of contact is the person in the publicity department assigned to work with your book. More than one work of insignificance has been turned into a nationwide best seller by the sheer stamina and promotional acumen of its creator.

Part II

PREPARING YOUR MANUSCRIPT

2
Manuscript Presentation

2.1 PAPER

Whenever you submit a manuscript to a publisher it should be typed on standard white bond 8½-by-11-inch typing paper (8-by-10-inch paper is adequate but not preferred; 8½-by-14-inch is *not* acceptable). All pages in the manuscript should be of uniform size, with no jutting edges. If using a printer, remove the perforation strips from the edges of all pages before submission. Do *not* use coated, erasable papers which are not friendly to the editor's pen markings, or onionskin papers which tend to crease easily during handling.

2.2 TYPING

Manuscripts must *always* be typewritten whenever submitted for publication. Exceptions will never be made. Double-space all copy including footnotes, references, bibliographies, lists, tables, extracts, captions, etc., and type on one side of the page only. Office machine copies of typed pages are perfectly acceptable, as long as they are clearly and not too darkly reproduced.

2.3 MARGINS AND SPACING

To facilitate editing leave 1-inch margins on the right, left, top, and bottom of the body text. All printed matter on the typed page should be kept within a 7-by-10-inch "image area." Chapter openings should start at least 3 inches from the top of the page. Right and left margins on pages bearing mathematical symbols are best set at 1½-inches for text and 2-inches for display work.

2.4 MANUSCRIPT LENGTH

The page length of your manuscript can be worked out with your publisher and then specified in your contract. Keep to this length as carefully as possible—an over-sized manuscript will dramatically raise the original estimated production costs of your book.

If you become aware during the course of writing that your book is running longer than the length specified in the contract, speak with an editor right away. At this point changes can still be made. An over-long manuscript delivered without adequate warning may force the editor to cut the book down to its originally agreed-upon size, a process that causes anguish for writer and editor alike. It's best to avoid the problem entirely by carefully planning out your chapter lengths in advance.

To estimate how many pages your typed manuscript will run when printed in book form, refer to Table 2-1. These figures are based on the use of a standard 12-point typewriter at approximately 300 words per page.

2.5 PAGE NUMBERING

When numbering your text, use regular Arabic numerals. Place all numbers in the upper right-hand corner of the page and number all pages consecutively, starting at the first page of the actual text (not from the title page, table of contents, etc.). If extra pages must be inserted into

Table 2-1.

Number of pages in typed manuscript	Approximate length in words	Approximate length of finished book
200	60,000	160
230	70,000	190
265	80,000	225
300	90,000	255
335	100,000	290
400	120,000	320
500	150,000	415

an already paginated manuscript, number these new pages with consecutively lettered numbers (for example, if you insert three extra pages after page 18, number these pages 18a, 18b, 18c, etc.).

2.6 FRONT MATTER

Your book should contain a title page (indicating both author and title) and a table of contents. Preface, dedication, acknowledgments, illustration list, epigraph, and biographical sketches, if included, should all be placed in front, ahead of the text.

2.7 TABLE OF CONTENTS

A standard table of contents displays the beginning page number of each section in the book. These sections include the front matter, text, appendix, glossary, index, etc. If your book is divided into major parts, these also should be indicated. Subheads within chapters should be included in the table of contents for technical works but are usually unnecessary in trade editions. For certain books, especially those which belong in that gray category between technical subjects and trade, a compromise may be in order using one level of subheads in the table but not two. If you have any questions on this potentially complicated matter consult your editor.

2.8 MOUNTING REPRINT COPY

Sometimes you may wish to attach previously printed materials—reprint copy—directly onto your manuscript. Cut out the items you wish to add and mount them neatly onto a standard 8½-x-11-inch page with rubber cement. Do not use either tape or staples for this job; the former cannot be written on in pen while the latter are notorious destroyers of felt-tip pens.

2.9 MAKING ON-PAGE CORRECTIONS

Make all corrections to the manuscript with a typewriter rather than a pen or pencil. Delete materials with a liquid correction fluid (such as Liquid Paper) and type in the changes. If numerous corrections must be made, retype the entire page. In general, try to keep the manuscript as presentable as possible. A neat manuscript makes the editor's job easier and hence speeds up production.

3
Style

3.1 SPELLING

Webster's *Collegiate* or Webster's *New International Dictionary* are considered to be the standard authorities on spelling, although any good dictionary can be consulted. Check all strange and unfamiliar words, as well as words commonly misspelled (e.g., calendar, cemetery, supersede, etc.). When an alternate spelling is listed in the dictionary, choose the word that is listed first unless the dictionary says plainly that the second spelling is preferred *in the specific sense in which you are using it*. For example, when writing about banking and home-loans the word *installment* is often spelled with a single *l*—instalment. This is a perfectly acceptable variant when used in this particular context.

3.2 CAPITALIZATION

Capitalization is one of the most complex of all style questions, and here we list only the most useful and important rules.

Capitalize the first word of each sentence, and of each line of regular poetry.

Capitalize the following proper names and abbreviations of proper names:

Names of people: George Washington, John Doe, Elmer Fudd

Formal names of places: India, Mount Snow, Action Park, the Lifey River

Names of ships, planes, trains: the Broadway Limited, the Queen Mary, the Spruce Goose

Political parties: Democrat, Whig, Conservative

Churches and their members: The Christian Science Church, a Muslim, a Mormon

Races: Mongolian, Caucasian

Documents: the Constitution, the Magna Carta

Companies: I.B.M., Rolls Royce, Paragon House

Trademarks and brand names: Chevrolet, Orlon, Xerox

Buildings: the Empire State Building, the Texas School Book Depository

Organizations and associations: the Boy Scouts of America, the N.A.A.C.P.

Institutions: Harvard College, the Smithsonian Institution

Languages: French, Urdu, Swedish

Names of awards and prizes: Nobel Prize, Guggenheim Fellowship

Also capitalize:

References to the Deity, sacred books, religious concepts, sacred figures and events: Siva, Him, the Old Testament, the Immaculate Conception, the Prophet Mohammad, the Diaspora

Titles of books, plays, magazines, musical compositions: *Love's Labors Lost*, *Life Magazine*, *Tender is the Night*, the *Ninth Symphony*. These should be typed as shown, upper and lower case, in italics or underlined. However, never type an entire title in capital letters, either for purposes of emphasis or for titling. Note too that the rules for capitalizing titles of foreign books differs somewhat from the standard rules; see section 3.5 "Foreign Words," for more information on this subject.

The titles of chapters, headings, subheadings, and sections of a written work: Chapter IV; The Legatee; His Rights; Section Seven

The names of the days, weeks, months, years, and holidays: Thursday, Mother's Day, January, Year of the Snake

Personal titles of rank, profession, or office when used with the name of the person: President Kennedy, Bishop Stuart, Mayor Beizer

Wars, battles, campaigns, and theaters of war: Operation Overlord, Maginot Line, War of Jenkin's Ear

A rule of thumb for capitalizing hyphenated compounds in titles is to: (1) always capitalize the first element and (2) capitalize the second element if it is a noun or proper adjective, or if it has equal force with the first element: Twentieth-Century Literature, City-State, Non-Christian. Do not capitalize the second element if: (1) it is a participle modifying the first element or (2) both elements constitute a single word: Self-sustaining Reaction, E-flat Minor, English-speaking People.

3.3 HYPHENATION

In order to improve a manuscript's clarity and appearance, avoid dividing words at the end of a line whenever possible. Indeed, it is generally better to leave a line of type slightly short or long at the right hand margin than to hyphenate it.

Prefixes and suffixes are usually closed up *without* a hyphen (e.g., multitone, precooled, substrata, semicircle). To avoid confusion, however, some exceptions are made, as in words like co-op, or when the letter *i* is repeated at the break, as in anti-inflationary. Use hyphens in most compound adjectives, such as in short-term loan, small-size edition, present-day ethics, ten-cent-store toys. Also, hyphenate when one component of a phrase is a cardinal number and the other a noun or adjective, as in nine-inch ruler, six-pointed star, one-sided affair. If you are uncertain how a word or phrase should be divided for hyphenation consult a good dictionary, such as Webster's *Collegiate*.

3.4 EMPHASIS

When you wish to emphasize an idea or call attention to a specific word, set it in italic (if your typewriter or printer allows) or underline it (underlining signifies to the typesetter that this word is to be set in italic). At the same time, be careful not to italicize too frequently—this valuable technique can easily lose its impact if over used. Entire sentences should seldom be italicized, and never a whole passage. Do not use boldface for emphasis when typing or printing out your material.

3.5 FOREIGN WORDS

Anglicized foreign words, i.e., foreign words which have become part of the English language, such as "agenda," "chili," "contralto," "ersatz," "kindergarten," and "ricochet" are never italicized. Non-Anglicized foreign words such as *auf Wiedersehen, dolce far niente, en rapport,* and *raison d'etre* are set in italic. Foreign proper names are not italicized, even when cited as foreign terms. If you are unsure whether or not a word is Anglicized, consult a dictionary.

Quotations from a foreign language should be set in quotations, not in italics. When capitalizing the titles of books, plays, and poems in foreign languages the rule of thumb is to capitalize only those words which would be capitalized in normal prose, e.g., the first word in the title, proper names, dates, etc. There are exceptions to this rule, however, specifically in German where nouns are capitalized and in Dutch where proper adjectives are capitalized. For the sometimes tricky particulars of punctuation and capitalization as it appears in specific foreign languages consult a good style manual, such as *The Chicago Manual of Style.*

3.6 NUMBERS

Spell out all cardinal numbers from one through ninety-nine. Numbers above ninety-nine are represented with numerical figures (e.g., More than 375 members were present at the meeting). The same rule applies to ordinary numbers (e.g.,

By the *eighth* of January we'd climbed to the *149th* position). However, note the exceptions: (1) when a group of small numbers are listed consecutively in the same sentence it may be cosmetically preferable to use figures instead of words (e.g., The ages of the horses are, respectively, 3, 4, 7, 11, and 13); (2) When a group of numbers belonging to the same category are listed in sequence, these numbers should be styled alike for consistency's sake whether these numbers are above 100 or below (e.g., There were 50 Russians, 115 Italians, 15 Poles, 130 English, and only 6 Americans present at the final awards ceremony).

No matter what the size of the number, if it comes at the beginning of a sentence it must be spelled out. Sometimes you may wish to avoid this awkward convention by simply rephrasing the sentence, especially if the number is a long or complex one. Round numbers and large numerical approximations should be spelled out (e.g., Here we are experiencing more than a *thousand* years of prejudice; It was estimated that at least *seven hundred* people died in the earthquake). For numbers in the millions and billions, the words *million* and *billion* are spelled out and their designating numbers are set in figures (e.g., The star is 25 *billion* light years away from our planetary system; At least

150 million people will be voting in the next election).

Numerals are used to indicate age in years, though casual references to periods in the life cycle such as "the thirties," are spelled out. Year numbers are invariably expressed in figures (e.g., Plato, we believe, died in 347 **B.C.**). References to centuries are spelled out, but if decades are identified by their century figures are used (e.g., In the 1880s the fighting began). Exact dates are written in the sequence of day–month–year, without internal punctuation (e.g., On 10 March 1942 a great event occurred in the nursery). If the alternate sequence, month–day–years, is used, the year is set off by commas before it and after it (e.g., The day of December 7, 1941, will live in infamy). Times of the day in even, half, and quarter hours are usually spelled out (e.g., We will meet at three o'clock), though figures must be used when the exact moment of time is to be emphasized (e.g., The movie starts at exactly 3:10 in the afternoon).

If an abbreviation or symbol is used for a unit of measure, its quantity should always be represented as a figure (e.g., 55 MPH; 177 km; 3½"). In most figures of four numbers or more, commas are inserted in between each group of three digits, starting from the first figure to the right (e.g., 35,900,338,321; 9,210; 21,000). Do not, however, place commas to the right of a decimal point, and do not use commas with binary digits, radio frequency designations, serial numbers, telephone numbers, or degrees of temperature.

3.7 TECHNICAL AND MATHEMATICAL COPY

Technical and mathematical copy must be clear, unambiguous, and fastidiously neat. All English characters and numerals used in equations are to be typewritten, preferably on a mathematics typewriter (if using a Selectric, avoid miniature subscript and superscript characters, as they do not duplicate well). Greek symbols and logic symbols should also be typewritten. If these are not available on your keyboard, be sure and write them clearly in ink.

Number all equations by a dual numbering system, chapter number listed first, equation number second. Numbered equations should then be "displayed," that is, set off from the text. If references are to be made to equations, refer to them by number and not by such phrases as "the equation below."

Mathematical signs are to be considered as substitutes for words, and all equations should be in grammatical sentence form. Simplify exponents if possible, and be wary of placing a subscript or superscript within another subscript or superscript. When possible, without obscuring meaning, use the solidus (/) with fractions to avoid spreading apart lines of type. If necessary, employ parentheses to preserve meaning.

Use standard notation whenever possible, the American National Standards Institute (ANSI) publishes a number of standards for letter symbols in various fields. If you must include unusual characters, signs, or symbols, list them clearly on a separate appended page for the editors to use (indicating the first and last pages on which they occur), along with an estimate of how many times each of these figures is listed.

3.8 SUBHEADINGS

Subheads are added to the text in order to: (1) help readers understand the organization of chapter material; (2) show important divisions within the text materials; and (3) indicate the subject matter to be discussed in the section that follows.

All important words in the subhead should be capitalized. Articles, conjunctions, and short prepositions are usually *not* capitalized unless they come at the beginning of the subhead. Note that the book designer will ultimately make the final decisions concerning how the subheads are set, whether in full capitals, in italic or roman, flush or centered.

Most texts require only one degree (level) of subhead throughout the text, the major exceptions being highly technical writings where two and even three levels are sometimes displayed. Subheads are usually set on a line separate from the text, the levels differentiated by type (size, capitals versus lower case, roman versus italic) and placement. The lowest level is often set at the beginning of the paragraph in italics, and is followed by a period. Always be consistent in your use and placement of subheads, and follow throughout the texts whatever precedents you have originally established, being careful to distinguish levels of heads clearly if more than one level is used. Subheads are a direct reflection of the way you choose to organize your material. Use them thoughtfully.

3.9 ENDNOTES

Most publishers advise against using footnotes, and many request that you use *endnotes* instead—notes placed at the end of the chapter or at the back of the book, *not* at the bottom of the page. Endnotes have several advantages over footnotes: their length is not limited by page space (though writers should be cautioned against compiling note sections so massive they overweigh the text), they are easier to find in the text, and they help avoid giving pages a cluttered look.

If possible, place endnotes at the back of the book; notes situated at the end of each chapter tend to be difficult to locate. However, a volume of essays in which each essay is contributed by a different author should have its notes placed appropriately at the conclusion of each essay. Authors must also avoid placing any "special note" at the bottom of a page marked with an asterisk, exceptions being, of course, manuscript notes addressed by the author to the editor.

Double-space all notes, using ordinary paragraph indentation. Endnotes should be placed in a section at the end of the book entitled "Notes" and should be arranged by chapters. For example:

Head—Notes

Subhead—Chapter 8

22. Cf. Bernard's *Tractatus de Cantu*, PL 182:1121.

23. On Henry, see WM, *De Nug Curm* 71, 289.

24. Damascus bribed the King of Jerusalem (with spurious coin) to retire.

Etc.

Notes for each chapter are numbered consecutively within the chapter, beginning with number one. Place all text note numbers at the end of the sentence, or if this is not possible, at the end of a clause. Note numbers should follow punctuation, rather than precede it. Note that numbers are typed above the line, with no parentheses, periods, or slash marks added. When quoting, the note number appears *after* the quote. A long quotation in an endnote is indented and punctuated in the same way that a regular textual extract or quotation is indented and punctuated. (See section 3.14, "Quotations.")

3.10 BIBLIOGRAPHIES

A good bibliography should include the following entries:

- · Names of the author or authors, the editors, or the institution responsible for writing the book.

- Full title of the book, including the subtitle, if any.
- Title of series, if any, and volume or number in the series
- Volume number or total number of volumes of a multivolume work
- Edition, if this is not the original
- City of publication
- Publisher's name
- Date of publication.

There are two basic styles of bibliographical entry. We shall refer to them as style A and B. Style A is favored by writers in the fields of literature, history, and the arts, style B by writers in the natural, physical, and social sciences. Either style—and sometimes a variation using elements of each—is acceptable when used *consistently* throughout the bibliography. Style A is as follows:

Rivers, John P. *Urban Blight: The Dynamics of Despair.* Carver City: Praxis Publishing Co., 1986.

Weimer, Mary. "Primate Eschatology: Apes and the Notion of an Afterlife." *Anthropoid Review* 6 (1984):133–146.

And style B:

Rivers, J.P. 1986. *Urban Blight: The Dynamics of Despair.* Carver City: Praxis.

Or:

Rivers, J.P. 1986. *Urban Blight.* Carver City: Praxis.

Weimer, M. 1984. "Primate Eschatology: Apes and the Notion of an Afterlife." *Anthropoid Rev.* 6: 133–146.

Or:

Weimer, M. 1984. "Primate Eschatology." *Anthropoid Rev.* 6: 133–146.

3.11 INDEX

According to the letter of most publishing contracts, authors are responsible for providing an index to their manuscript. As a rule, however, publishers understand that writers feel considerably under the gun while preparing a publication-length book and in many instances they will be willing to help the writer avoid the tedious job of preparing an index by hiring a professional indexer. In any event, indexing is a matter that should be discussed with an editor before you begin work, and arrangements for it should ideally be spelled out clearly in your contract.

A good index includes both proper names and subject entries. Occasionally, when the subject matter is far-ranging and the book includes many names, places, theories, incidents, etc., two indexes will be necessary, one for people, the other for subjects.

When deciding which material to index, assume that most of the front matter (title, dedications, epigraph, etc.) will not be included. The preface should be indexed only if it pertains significantly to the subject of the book itself and is not simply an explanation of why and how the book was written. Using file cards when assembling index material is an extremely helpful technique and is highly recommended.

3.12 TABLES

Tables must be supplied both in the text itself *and* on a separately attached sheet of paper, with each table on this sheet keyed to its corresponding page number in the text. All tables are to be double-spaced and identified by a system of double numbering, the first number indicating the chapter, the second indicating the table's sequential place within that chapter (*e.g.*, a sequence of tables in Chapter 12 would read: Table 12.1, Table 12.2, Table 12.3, etc.). Title all tables briefly and clearly, and be certain that the numbering sequences for tables and illustrations are kept separate.

Table titles should not furnish background information or describe the results illustrated in the table. Such explanations are to be placed in footnotes at the bottom of the table, but only when absolutely necessary. When composing the table title be concise, and use participles rather than relative clauses. Here, for instance, is an example of right wording and wrong wording. This title is for a table that lists the number of professional athletes who contribute to charitable causes:

Right: Athletes Contributing to Charitable Causes

Wrong: Number of Athletes who Contribute to Charitable Causes

All titles should be placed at the top of the table, and all columns must be carefully aligned. Footnotes are set directly below the table, their width matching the width of the table. Table titles are typed on the line(s) below the identifying number, with only the first letters of important words capitalized. Tables should be referred to throughout the text by specific number, not by such vague phrases as "the table that follows" or "as indicated in the table below."

3.13 CROSS-REFERENCES

Whenever possible, avoid making cross-references to other pages in your manuscript. Why? Because the exact page numbers to which these references refer cannot be filled in by the editor until late in the production process, and delays may result. Refer instead to specific chapters, subsections, tables, charts, pictures, etc., making sure that these materials are numbered and that you refer to them by their specific numbers (e.g., See Figure 5.3). Exception: subsections do not *have* to be numbered and can be referred to by title.

3.14 QUOTATIONS

All quotations must *precisely* reproduce the wording, the spelling, and the punctuation of the source quoted. Look on all quotes as photographic images of the original. Possible exceptions allow for modernizing the spelling of older works, correcting typographical errors, and capitalizing the initial letter of an uncapitalized sentence.

Generally speaking, all one- or two-line quotations should stay within the body text. Quotes that go on for four or five lines (or more) should be indented and set off from the text. Double-space these longer quotes as a single block paragraph, and leave extra space both above and below the block.

Words and phrases that introduce quoted material, such as "thus" or "the following items," are usually followed by a colon. Quoted poetry is always centered on the page. Its spacing and punctuation reproduces the original poem exactly.

Material set off from the text as a block quotation is *not* placed in quotation marks. However, any quoted material that comes as part of the text within the block should be enclosed in double quotation marks, even if the source quoted uses only single marks. Moreover, the first sentence of a block quotation can either be indented or set flush to the left, at the author's whim. Just be consistent. (The most common practice is to base all punctuation on the quote itself. That is, if the first line of the quoted material is indented, indent the block quotation too.) Quotations in foreign languages are not italicized and are punctuated the same way as regular quotations in English. Finally, be selective when choosing materials to include in your quotes, especially when reproducing an interview. Every "uh" and "you know?" is not required reading. Replace extraneous parts of speech, throat clearings, and grunts with ellipses or, better yet, eliminate them completely.

3.15 RACISM, OBSCENITIES, CRUDE LANGUAGE

All of the above are appropriate in a manuscript only when they are intrinsic to the story or text, that is, when they are featured as quoted materials or as part of a dramatic dialogue. Authors should refrain from imposing their opinions on readers concerning such topics as racism, either directly or by inference, unless the text deals specifically with these matters. The inclusion of gratuitous obscenities in the course of normal explication is unwarranted and out of place.

3.16 SEXIST LANGUAGE

Avoid it. The following examples show how a little judicious rewriting can turn sexist usage into acceptable prose:

> It was truly a *man-sized* task that faced us.
> It was truly an enormous (monumental,

whopping, staggering, humongous, Brobding-
nagian, etc.) task that faced us.

The judge then makes *his* final speech and
summons the jury.
After then delivering a final speech, the
judge summons the jury.

We flew the plane in and banked *her* to the
right.
We flew the plane in and banked it to the
right.

A physicist should never be without *his*
slide rule.
A physicist should never be without a slide
rule.
A physicist should never be without his or
her slide rule.

Mrs. King and Riggs volleyed for serve.
King and Riggs volleyed for serve.

We'll have our *girl* take notes during the
meeting.
We'll have our assistant take notes during
the meeting.

The pioneers moved west, taking *their
wives and children* with them.
Pioneer families moved west.

3.17 USING STYLE GUIDE REFERENCE BOOKS

If questions of style arise that are not answered in this manual, writers are urged to consult standard style guides first such as *The Chicago Manual of Style* or *Words Into Type,* rather than to rely on their better judgment. In matters of style and grammar, what seems to be the most efficient and logical way is not always the accepted way.

4
Drawings, Photographs, Charts, and Graphs

4.1 PERMISSIONS, FEES, AND CREDITS

Unless terms in your contract stipulate otherwise, the following responsibilities belong to the author: (1) to locate whatever art work, photographs, paintings, drawings, illustrations, etc., are to be included in the text, (2) to gain written permission from the owner/s for the use of this artwork, (3) to hire artists, illustrators, and/or photographers when original artwork must be produced, and (4) to negotiate and pay all fees for these items.

Usually, the artist or photographer owns the reproduction rights to his or her own work, especially for photographs taken since 1978, when tighter copyright laws were introduced. Send your permission requests directly to these individuals or, if necessary, to the picture agency, museum, publisher, foundation, newspaper, etc., that controls the rights. Do so well in advance of publication date, ideally before finishing the final draft of the manuscript, as the process of gaining permission is often a slow one.

When a fee is requested, decide whether the material is worth the asking price. If you think it is, the fee should be paid according to the method agreed upon in your contract (the best deal for the author and publisher is to have the permissions fee payable on publication of the book), and a copy of the letter granting permissions should be sent to your publisher. Note too that the owners of the art work will ordinarily want a credit line exhibited on their illustrations. This credit should always be worded (within reason) in accord with the owner's wishes. Credit lines are generally supplied in the caption accompanying the illustration. For more information on permissions see section 9 below, "Permissions."

4.2 PREPARING THE ILLUSTRATIONS

All art work, drawings, graphs, diagrams, photographs, etc. must be given to the publisher in the forms of originals, not office machine copies or stats. Illustrations should be delivered camera-ready, either as professionally drafted originals or as glossies of originals. If it is not possible to provide originals, inform your editor of this fact *before* sending in the material. In such cases, photostats may be acceptable; xeroxes usually are not.

All photographs should be 5-by-7 or 8-by-10 black-and-white halftones. Avoid submitting color slides or color prints to be reproduced as black-and-white halftones. Illustrations are usually delivered along with the finished manuscript.

When preparing your manuscript for submission insert photo copies of the illustrations into the appropriate places in the text, and make sure all artwork is accompanied by a separate list of captions. Do not type captions onto the manuscript or onto the illustrations; type them double-spaced on a separate list and submit this along with the illustrations, making sure all captions are correctly keyed to the pictures and text.

Double-number all artwork with Arabic numerals according to the order in which the artwork appears in each chapter. For example, the first illustration in Chapter 6 will be 6.1, the second 6.2, and so on. Every line drawing and photograph must be identified when submitted, preferably by a typewritten label affixed to its back. The following information should be included on this label:

- The title of the book
- The author's name
- The title of the illustration (or a brief description)
- The name of the artist/photographer
- The name of the permissions holder
- The illustration's number in the text
- The number of the page on which the illustration appears

Never mark the back of an illustration with a pen, and *never* attach anything to it with a staple or paperclip. Always use labels. The best method of all is to slip the original illustration into a glassine envelope and attach the identifying label onto this envelope.

When labels, arrows, and cropping instructions must be added to an illustration, place these marks on a transparent overlay, and tape (don't staple or clip) the overlay to the front of the picture. Write lightly on the overlay with a soft pencil or felt tip pen to avoid making an imprint on the artwork.

4.3 SUBMISSION AND RETURN OF ART MATERIALS

Package all artwork separately from the manuscript and make sure it is clearly marked—more than one envelope of illustrations has gone astray due to improper labeling. Small drawings are to be submitted on separate sheets. Large drawings should be rolled, not folded. Deliver photographs flat, and keep a photocopy of original illustrations for your records, along with an inventory list of all submitted artwork. If sending materials through the mail, post them as registered mail to insure proper handling.

Ordinarily, all artwork will be kept by a publisher until publication. Until that time original prints, illustrations, etc. cannot usually be returned. While every measure will, of course, be taken by the publisher to safeguard your illustrated materials, there is always an element of risk involved, and it is suggested that you keep duplicates of all irreplaceable photographs and important materials.

5
Responsibilities of Editors of Contributed Volumes

The editor of a contributed volume—e.g., a volume of essays or selected writings contributed by different authors—faces a special challenge: to take the disparate points of view espoused by these writers and turn the collection into a cohesive whole. Each contributing author, of course, should follow the guidelines presented in this book, and should carefully prepare his or her portion of the manuscript for submission. The volume editor then takes all these individual essays and checks them over carefully, making certain that:

- All text is neatly typed and complete.
- Tables and illustrations have been supplied (see section 3.12 "Tables" above).
- All permissions for illustrations and quotations have been granted, all permissions fees negotiated or paid, and all credit lines supplied.
- The book's content is in good order. Are there problems with the book's structure or style? Is the subject matter time-sensitive, and if so, is the essay dated? Does each essay fit into the scheme of the volume as a whole? Will any rewriting be necessary?
- In the case of books that reprint conference proceedings, all extraneous niceties from speeches made during the course of the

conference are removed (such as: "Today, ladies and gentlemen, we have discussed many significant issues . . . ")

- All mention of dates that can brand a manuscript as obsolete are removed.

In addition to the above, the volume editor must review the collection as a whole in order to:

- Compile a captions and illustrations list.
- Check the table of contents against the first page of each essay in order to resolve inconsistencies in chapter titles and/or spellings of authors' names.
- Check for consistency of documentation. Ideally, all essays will follow the same documentation format and style. The volume editor decides on an appropriate documentation style and may ask contributors to revise their documentation in accordance with this style. (See sections 3.9 "Endnotes" and 3.10 "Bibliographies.")

· Call the in-house editor's attention, by letter or memo, to any matter requiring special treatment in the manuscript (e.g., unusual type characters or symbols, complex illustrations, idiosyncratic spelling or usage, etc.).

After the manuscript has been copyedited, it will be sent to the volume editor. The volume editor then reviews the manuscript and checks its overall appearance. The volume editor is responsible for distributing the copyedited essays to the various contributors and for making sure that all queries are thoroughly answered. In like manner, the volume editor makes sure that each contributor receives his or her typeset galleys for proofreading or assumes responsibility for proofreading them, depending on the stipulations in the contract. (Consult an in-house editor.) Finally, the volume editor monitors the schedules for return of these materials, and sees to it that the complete volume is returned to the publisher (in one shipment) according to the deadline set by the editorial and production staff.

6
Delivering the
Final
Manuscript

When your manuscript is ready to be submitted try, if possible, to have it hand-delivered to the publisher. If hand-delivery is not feasible, carefully secure the manuscript and art work in separate boxes, using stiff cardboard and strong wrapping paper, and send both parcels registered or insured. *Always*, repeat *always* retain a machine copy of the originals for your records.

Make every attempt to submit your manuscript on time. Prompt compliance with delivery terms, as spelled out in your contract, will make the job easier for a publisher's editorial staff and will help get your book out and selling in the stores that much sooner. If for whatever reason the completion of your book must be delayed, inform the editor concerning this fact well in advance of the delivery date so you can negotiate the necessary extension of the manuscript delivery deadline specified in your contract.

Part III

PRODUCTION AND PUBLICATION OF YOUR MANUSCRIPT

7
Preparing Your Manuscript for Publication

7.1 THE COPYEDITED MANUSCRIPT

After you submit your completed manuscript to a publisher the text will be carefully checked over for details of punctuation, spelling, syntax, usage, content, etc. by a copyeditor. The copyedited manuscript will then be returned to you for review.

Go over all corrections carefully, adding

your own changes and corrections when necessary. Now is the time to make these changes. Later, when you receive the printed galleys, last minute alterations *can* be made, but they will be expensive, both for the publisher and, in certain instances, for the author as well. (See section 7.3, "Reading and Correcting the Galleys.") It is better to do as much of the editing work as possible now, at this early stage.

Table 7-1 will help you become more conversant with the copyeditor's markings.

When marking a copyedited manuscript make sure that all corrections are clearly and precisely written. Correct with a pen, not with a pencil, and make sure that your pen's color is different from the colors already marked on the manuscript. If you make a mistake, cover it with liquid paper; don't cross it out. Make all corrections directly on the manuscript. Do not submit a list of corrections. Any lengthy insertions should be typed on separate sheets and attached to the page on which they are to be inserted.

If a manuscript page is so heavily marked up that it becomes difficult to read, retype the entire page separately, taking care to incorporate all of the copyeditor's original changes. Attach the new page to the old and return both.

Table 7-1 Copyeditor's Markings

MARK	EXPLANATION and/or EXAMPLE	MARK	EXPLANATION and/or EXAMPLE
⊙	Insert period ∧		Lower Case with Initial Capitals
⌃ or ,/	Insert comma ∧		SET IN small capitals
⊙ or :/	Insert colon ∧		SMALL CAPITALS WITH INITIAL CAPITALS
; /	Insert semicolon ∧	rom.	Set in roman type
✌ or ℣/	Apostrophe, boys	ital.	Set in italic type
℣/ ℣℣	Insert quotation marks ∧	ital caps	ITALIC Capitals or ═══
? /	Insert question mark ∧	l.f.	Set in lightface type
! /	Insert exclamation point ∧	b.f.	Set in boldface type
= /	Insert hyphen =	bf. italic	Boldface italic
$\frac{1}{en}$	En dash ∧	b.f. Caps	BOLDFACE capitals or ═══
$\frac{1}{em}$	One-em dash ∧	☟	Superior letter or figure ∧
$\frac{3}{em}$	Three-em dash ∧	☝	Inferior letter or figure, HO
(/)	Insert parentheses ∧¹∧	ℋ	Begin a paragraph
[/]	Insert brackets ∧ one ∧	no ℋ	No paragraph ⌐
´	Set pri ∧ mar´ y accent	run in	└ Run in or run on
″	Set sec´ on dar ∧ y accent	□ ℋ	Indent the number of em quads shown
⌒ or lig	Use ligature (oe, ae, fi, etc.)	flush	No indention
/	Virgule, slash; and/or	hanging indent	Hanging indention. Mark all lines to ⌐ desired indention.
○○○○○	Leaders (6 unit spacing)		
. . . . . .	Leaders (3 dot, tight space)	O C or out copy	Insert matter omitted; refer to copy (Mark copy Out, see proof, galley 00)
●○○○●	Ellipsis (6 unit spacing) . . .		
⊗ or X	Replace broken or marred type	∧	Caret. Insert marginal addition
◡	Reverse (turn type or cut)	ℐ or ℐ	Dele. Take out (delete) ℐ
SP	Spell out (twenty gr.) grain	ℐ	Delete and close up
(Q ? Ed.)	Query to editor	e /	Correct letter or word marked
⌐	Mark-off or break; start new line	stet	Let it stand—(all matter above dots)
wf	Wrong font	] or pts	Move to right (How many points?)
wfs	wrong font size	[or pts	Move to left (How many points?)
lc	Lower Case or LOWER CASE	⌐ /	Lower (letters or words)
C	capital letter	⌐ ⌐	Elevate (letters or words)
Caps	SET IN capitals	⟋	Straighten line (horizontally)
‖ or ⌐	Align type (vertically)	◡	Close up entirely; take out space
tr	Transpose space	⊛	Close up partly; leave some space
tr	Transpose enclosed in ring (matter)	✓ or ⌃	Less space between words
tr	Transpose (order letters of or words)	⌃ or eq#	Equalize space between words
tr	Rearrange words of order numbers in	l / s	LETTER-SPACE (Usually 1 unit extra)
center	Put in center of line or page (ctr)	#	Insert space (or more space)
⌐ ℐ ⌐	Center line for line	space out	More space between words

69

7.2 ANSWERING THE EDITOR'S QUERIES

Editors will always have questions concerning both the style and content of a manuscript. These questions will be indicated by editorial notes written in the margins, or more commonly by notated flags (flags are small gummed tabs which are attached to the queried pages). Answer all questions carefully, keeping in mind the fact that many flags added to a manuscript are an indication of an editor's thoroughness, *not* that your manuscript is in any way deficient.

7.3 READING AND CORRECTING THE GALLEYS

After you correct and return the copyedited manuscript your book will be typeset into galley proofs. A set of these proofs will then be sent to you for final corrections. Mark corrections directly on the galleys, with a brightly colored pen. Do *not* submit a list of corrections. Know, at this point, that every change made in these galleys *requires the resetting of at least one full line of type and sometimes, if the correction is lengthy (i.e., if it introduces more than a few extra characters) or comes in the middle of a paragraph, many full lines.* It is thus extremely important that you make changes on the galley proofs *only* when they are absolutely essential. Make changes only when:

1) There is an obvious printing error in spelling, punctuation, etc.
2) A fact or figure is incorrect.
3) In rare cases, essential new material must be added (although note: if you intend to add new material at this stage be sure to consult with an editor first).

When adding changes to the galley proofs, attention to the mechanics of typesetting can reduce costs considerably. For instance, if you are replacing a word in the middle of a sentence, replace it with another single word, not with a long phrase; and better still, replace it with a word that has the same number of letters as the word replaced. If possible, make your changes at the end of a paragraph rather than in the middle. If you need to add one or more new sentences add them to the end of the paragraph, not to the beginning. (Another approach is to place these additions into a new and separate paragraph.) By following these methods the need to reset typed lines can be considerably reduced.

71

7.4 ALTERATION CHARGES TO THE AUTHOR

Errors made by the typesetter are corrected at the typesetter's expense. *All* other changes must be paid for. Who receives the bill? As a rule, the publisher will pay for typesetting changes up to 10 percent of the cost of setting the manuscript into type. Alterations in excess of the 10 percent must be charged to the author. However, bear in mind that the cost of resetting *one line* can be as high as $1.50, and that most corrections will involve resetting more than one line. Thus, costs can mount quickly. The rule of thumb is: correct galley proofs *only* when necessary.

7.5 SELLING RIGHTS TO YOUR BOOK

During the period of time when your book is being edited and typeset the publisher and/or your agent will be attempting to sell the book's subsidiary rights. What are these rights and how are they sold? In brief, as follows:

A. *Serial Rights.* These refer to the purchase of passages or extracted chapters from a book by a newspaper, journal, or magazine. "First serial rights" means that the right to print these new materials is offered for the first time—it has never before appeared in a magazine or newspaper. "Second serial rights" are sold after the book has been published and they usually bring considerably less money.

B. Syndication Rights. A newspaper may wish to publish excerpts from your book in a series of installments, say one installment every week for six weeks. The publisher (or sometimes the agent) will negotiate with the syndicator for "syndication rights," with the proceeds from the sale being divided up three ways, between author, publisher, and syndicator.

C. Dramatic, Television and Motion Picture Rights. If your manuscript has dramatic or documentary potential, and if a TV or film production company becomes interested, they will negotiate with the publisher and/or agent for dramatic rights. Sometimes producers will also purchase an "option" on your book, which means that you as author sell them a certain period of exclusive time—usually a year—in which to raise production money to finance the film. The sale of dramatic rights can be extremely lucrative and hence extremely complex, and it's a wise policy to let an experienced agent handle all such negotiations.

D. Foreign Serial Rights. Once your book's serial rights have been sold in the United States they can be peddled again an indefinite number of times practically anywhere in the world. Most foreign serial rights these days are sold to Canada, England, Australia, France, Germany, other countries in Europe, and to Japan.

Part IV

LEGAL CONCERNS FOR AUTHORS

8
Copyright

8.1 WHAT IS COPYRIGHT?

A copyright is a legal right designed to protect authors from the pirating and plagarizing of their materials. Copyright is normally procured by the publisher for the author in his or her name, and records of the transaction are kept on file at the publisher's office. Current copyright law protects the unpublished typed manuscript along with the finished book, which means that as soon as a copyright is procured the author's work is protected, no matter at what stage of production it happens to be.

8.2 WHAT DOES A COPYRIGHT PROTECT?

Current copyright laws protect the author in the following way:

- Books written after January 1, 1978 are covered by the copyright for the author's life plus fifty years.
- Works published prior to January 1, 1978, are protected by copyright for twenty-eight years from the date of publication, after which the copyright must be renewed to obtain an additional forty-seven years—a total of seventy-five years copyright protection.
- The copyright law allows you the right as author to print, reprint, sell, record and tape record, distribute, translate, novelize, and dramatically adapt your work in any way you see fit. You also have the right to sell your copyright privileges, should you receive such an offer. The Copyright Office in Washington (Library of Congress,

Washington, D.C. 20559) offers
a free copyright information kit.
Send for it if you desire more
information.

9
Permissions

9.1 RESPONSIBILITY FOR PERMISSIONS

Obtaining permissions and paying for the use of printed or illustrative materials is ordinarily the author's responsibility. This obligation pertains not only to borrowed passages and illustrations but to all tables, charts, graphs, photos, and lists.

9.2 GETTING PERMISSIONS

Copyright information will almost always be displayed on the back of a book's title page or, in magazines and journals, at the bottom of the table of contents. Write to the publisher, not the author, when seeking permissions. The publisher will ordinarily represent the author, will have all the pertinent copyright information on record, and will usually respond to your inquiries in a reasonable amount of time. If your letter isn't answered after a month, send a second request (a xeroxed copy of the first letter). If the second request isn't answered, send a third letter by certified mail, return receipt requested. This will prove your good faith in trying to find the owner of the material, should you and your publisher jointly decide to go ahead and use the material.

If you plan to alter or change any borrowed material, inform the copyright holders of your intentions; they may wish to see a copy of the altered material before permission is granted. Start writing for permissions well ahead of the time you submit your final manuscript. (It is a good idea to compile a list of needed permissions as you write your manuscript.) The process of gaining rights is often a sluggish one, and you will certainly want to know where you stand with the permission-grantor before your book goes to press. A sample permissions letter that can be adapted to fit the circumstances of any book, article, or illustration is reproduced in Figure 9-1 below. Send copies of this letter in duplicate to the copyright holder.

Note that copyright holders often specify the precise wording of the credit lines they desire as a provision of granting permissions. When this is the case, be sure to comply with their exact wishes.

Figure 9-1
Permissions Letter

Your address
The date

Name of permissions holder
Permission holder's address

Dear Sirs:

I am in the process of writing a book which is entitled _____ and which is intended to be used for _____. The book is scheduled for publication by the publisher in spring/summer/fall/winter of _____. I would like to procure permission from you to include in my book, and in all future editions and translations of my book, the following material from _____ by the author _____. A release form is provided below for your convenience.

Specifically, I would like to quote/reproduce all materials on pages _____ through _____. The passage starts on page _____ with the words "Once upon a time," and ends on page _____ with the words "happily ever after." A total of _____ words is included. It is understood, of course, that I will acknowledge your kindness in granting permissions in my book, and that full credit will be given to the author and publisher, either as a footnote or as a reference within the text. If you do not specify a specific credit line in the section provided below, I will prepare one according to the usual practice. If you do not hold these rights, please let me know to whom I should apply.

Thank you for your help and consideration. I will be grateful for an early reply, and I enclose a duplicate copy of this letter for your records.

Sincerely,

Name

I (we) hereby grant permission for the use of the material requested above:

Date _____   Signature _____

                      Title _____

Copyright credit line wished _____

9.3 WHEN PERMISSION IS DENIED

In those unusual instances where permission is denied, the author should locate other equivalent sources. Under no circumstances should any material be used without permission unless it falls under the domain of "fair use" (see section 10.1, "The Limits of Fair Use.") Unauthorized use can cause legal problems, sometimes serious ones, for both author and publisher. Be sure and give copies of your permission inquiries and responses to the editor when you hand in the final manuscript, and keep all originals for your files.

10
Fair Use

10.1 THE LIMITS OF FAIR USE

Sometimes you may wish to quote small, incidental passages from a particular book or article without going through the trouble of seeking permissions. This can be risky business, and it is always best to gain formal permission. However, under the fair use law a limited amount of material can be quoted without authorization. While just how much material can be used—how many words, how long a passage—has never been established, the fair use section of the copyright law reads as follows:

> 107. *Limitations on exclusive rights*: Fair use ... the fair use of a copy-

righted work . . . for purposes such as criticism, comment, news reporting . . . scholarship, or research, is not an infringement of copyright. In determining whether the use made of a work in any particular case is fair use the factors to be considered shall include—

(1) the purpose and character of the use, including whether such use is of a commercial nature or is for nonprofit educational purposes;
(2) the nature of the copyrighted work;
(3) the amount of substantiality of the portion used in relation to the work as a whole; and
(4) the effect of the use upon the potential market for or value of the copyrighted work.

Fair use does *not* cover quotations from a poem or from the lyrics of a song, even if these passages are only one or two lines long. Nor does it apply to material taken from unpublished manuscripts, anthologized works, charts, graphs, maps, art work, photographs, or quotes from published or unpublished letters. Also, be careful of taking quotes out of context and using them to establish points that are not proven (or sometimes not even implied) in the original quoted material.

Since permissions fees are almost always smaller than lawyers' fees, disputes over fair use seldom, if ever, get to court. Remember this rule of thumb: 300–500 words from an average-sized book (over 200 pages) can be used without requesting permission.

10.2 SPEECHES, INTERVIEWS, NEWSPAPER COPY

Speeches by government officials are in the public domain, but unpublished speeches delivered by private individuals require permission. The same holds true for interview materials—permission is almost always required, and this includes public interviews (even those made on television) as well as private interviews carried out for a specific book or article. Finally, newspaper copy such as articles, editorials, special reports, etc., is generally copyrighted, though the actual information provided in such pieces is public domain. In fact, most published information is public domain and can be freely reproduced, but only if the wording is sufficiently changed from the original.

10.3 WHAT CONSTITUTES LIBEL?

Libel is an attack on the reputation and good name of a living person. It can be any written or spoken words that injure a person's public standing or diminish the esteem and confidence in which that person is held by society. Libel may involve slander, invasion of privacy, or both. Representative examples include calling a person a "traitor to her country" when that person has never been legally convicted of such an act; publishing unauthorized, intimate quotes from a person's diary or correspondence; revealing tawdry and embarrassing facts about a person's sex life; incorrectly accusing a person of cruel, immoral, or illegal behavior. If authors are unsure whether or not passages in their manuscripts are potentially libelous they should consult with an editor, who will probably in turn consult with a lawyer to "vet" the book and remove any parts that look as if they might cause legal problems. "Vetting" a book can cost thousands of dollars and is usually worthwhile only on books that can generate substantial income. Many publishers will automatically avoid books that have potential for legal problems.

Part V

SPECIAL
CONCERNS

11
Converting the Thesis into Book Form

11.1 TONE

For those who are converting their thesis into a published manuscript certain cautions may be in order. First and foremost, remember that your book will now be read not only by colleagues, students, and members of the academic community but by the public at large; and that hence, all attempts should be made to keep your writing clear of both pedantry and obscurity.

Avoid what has rightly been called "the tyranny of facts." That is, keep your footnotes and quotations down to a reasonable number. Don't overload text with endless examples. Use tables, charts, and graphs *only* when they make the point better than direct exposition. Avoid complex cross-references. When you include passages from a foreign language, supply translations along with them. Include only appropriate books in your bibliography. Keep all notes simple. Don't go into lengthy descriptions of facts that are already obvious. Don't pad.

Further: avoid both apologetic introductions and musings on your own insufficiency. You are an expert in your field: write with confidence. At the same time, beware of dogmatism and of a patronizing attitude. The latter will be quickly noted by all intelligent readers and will subtly prejudice them against whatever it is you have to say.

11.2 STYLE

Avoid writing in the passive voice. The present and simple past tenses are best. Excessive use of auxiliary verbs serves only to slow down the read.

Vary your style. Inject occasional questions. Diversify your sentence structures. If your sentences tend to be long, balance them with short, pithy sentences. Create color with interesting, evocative verbs and adjectives. Use an occasional, well-chosen metaphor or anecdote when the opportunity is right. Strive to be interesting.

One of the major sins of thesis writing is over-writing. Condense and amalgamate whenever possible. If in doubt, cut. Go over your manuscript with a cruel eye and cross out absolutely *everything* that is repetitious or unnecessary. Especially avoid the "announcer" effect. That is, the use of phrases that loudly proclaim what you are about to say, or what you have already done:

> "We shall now proceed to a consideration of . . . "
> "In an earlier section of this work we learned that . . ."

Avoid also any unnecessary recapitulation.

> "As mentioned in Chapters 6 and 8, we see yet again that . . . "
> "This tendency, to remind the reader once more, is . . . "

Likewise, refrain from over use of the first person singular:

> "My major thrust in this work so far has been . . . though elsewhere I have dealt with . . . and here I feel it is important to go on record concerning my notion that . . . "

And, of course, don't brag:

> "Some years ago in a prize-winning essay I put forth the theory that . . . "
> "Having come up with Tillier's concept a decade before Tillier himself, I reasoned that . . . "

Always opt for clarity. Abstruse, scholarly words have their place, but make sure they are in their *right* place—obscure vocabulary used for its own sake smacks of pedantry. Likewise, avoid the cliche, along with all academic jargon and buzz words. In all, your goal should be to affect a writing style that communicates in a manner that is at once selective, self-assured, insightful, vivid, and personable—reread and correct from this simple perspective and you won't go wrong.

12 Guidelines for the Use of Word Processors

12.1 DO'S AND DON'TS ON THE COMPUTER

More and more writers are using word processors these days, and this means that an entire group of compositional caveats have arisen in conjunction with this new invention. A few of the more important ones include:

- Do not hand in a manuscript that has been justified on the right hand margin. Ragged right hand margins are best.
- Do remove the perforated edges from all printer typing paper before handing in your manuscript. Do not leave the typed pages attached in their continuous-feed mode; separate and collate each page before giving it to the publisher.
- Do be heedful of page breaks when formatting your material. Avoid placing subheadings at the bottom of pages with no text beneath them. If possible, use a word processor such as *Wordstar* that announces where page breaks occur.
- Do avoid leaving orphans whenever possible (an orphan is the last word of a paragraph which, because of careless formatting, appears as a single word on the following page).
- Do avoid placing note numbers on the line/s following their actual reference. Keep all note

numbers as close as possible to the reference itself.

· Do use superscripts to type in note numbers if this function is included in your printer's graphics capabilities. Do use the italics function if it is included in your printer and word processor.

· Do remember to turn on the page numbering function in your word processor.

· Do keep your manuscript on disc until the book has been published. Sometimes last minute revisions may be necessary, in which case having the manuscript on disc will make your job considerably easier and quicker. Some writers prefer to keep manuscript discs intact and on file for several years, on the chance that an update or a rewrite of their book will be commissioned. If you follow this wise practice make sure you label all discs carefully before storing them, and that you keep discs in a cool, dry, protected place away

from all stray telephone hookups
and electrical currents.

12.2 PRINTERS

Several years ago dot matrix printers hammered
out such shoddy print that they were judged by
most publishers to be unacceptable for the
printing of professional quality manuscripts.
Printer technology has improved a great deal
since that time and today documents typed in
LQ (Letter Quality) or NLQ (Near Letter Quality) dot matrix printers are perfectly acceptable.
As with any typewritten manuscript, however,
please be sure that the ribbon you use is fresh,
and that all spacings, margins, etc. are accurate.

With the development of new technologies
for manuscript typesetting, some publishers
may be willing to accept a manuscript on a
floppy disk. Consult your in-house editor with
inquiries about software, standards, and coding.

SUGGESTED READINGS

Applebaum, Judith and Nancy Evans. *How to Get Happily Published: A Complete and Candid Guide.* New York: New American Library, 1982.

R.R. Bowker Co. *Literary Market Place, 1988.* New York: R.R. Bowker Co., 1987.

Dessauer, John. *Book Publishing: What It Is, What It Does.* 2nd ed. New York: R.R. Bowker Co., 1981.

Fulton, Len, ed. *Directory of Small Magazine Press Editors and Publishers.* 18th ed. Paradise, CA: Dustbooks, 1987.

Huenefeld, John. *The Huenefeld Guide to Book Publishing.* Bedford, MA: The Huenefeld Co., Inc., 1986.

Johnston, Donald. *Copyright Handbook.* 2nd ed. New York: R.R. Bowker Co., 1982.

Peters, Jean, ed. *Bookman's Glossary.* 6th ed. New York: R.R. Bowker Co., 1983.

Skillen, M. and R. Gay. *Words Into Type.* 3rd ed. New York: Prentice-Hall, 1974.

University of Chicago. *Chicago Manual of Style.* 13th ed. Chicago: University of Chicago Press, 1982.